Dear one,

Talk to God.

Johnnie
Coleman
vi

OPEN YOUR MIND
AND BE HEALED

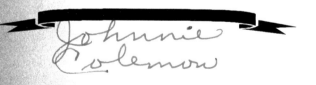

Wherever you are,

God is.

Johnnie
Colemon

Open
Your Mind
and Be
Healed

JOHNNIE COLEMON, D.D., D.H.L.

Foreword by
Della Reese

DeVorss Publications

"Called to Be Eagles," by James Aggrey, used by permission of Tyndale House Publishers, Inc. (pp. 77–79).

DeVorss & Company, *Publisher*
P.O. Box 550
Marina del Rey, CA 90294

C O N T E N T S

Foreword

A s A grateful student blessed to study with this extremely great expression of God, as a buddy and confidant, I am privileged to have seen this woman work in her life the principles she espouses. Seeing how well they worked for her and those she taught (who exercised these principles), I had to try them for myself, and she's absolutely correct when she says, "It Works If You Work It."

Intuitively we all know deep down inside these principles, but we are not always "consciously aware" of them when we need be. Dr. Colemon teaches us the art and science of our consciousness, our sense of awareness, our sense of knowing, the realization of who and what we are not only in an intellectual sense but also in a spiritually effective and active state, incorporated with the divine ideas necessary to manifest the life more abundantly that Jesus Christ came to bring us.

We are so much more than we think we are. We can do and be so much more than we think we can with so much less struggle and stress, anxiety and regret, if we are willing to raise the level of our consciousness, if we will "open our mind and be healed." Dr. Colemon can show you how. She showed me how when a blood vessel burst in my brain and I had two brain operations in ten days, and ten days later I was doing a commercial for Campbell's Soup.

This book is a blessing from God to improve your life and the lives of those who love you and all those who come in contact with you as they see you rise to your highest good.

This is a woman dedicated to raising the consciousness of thousands, week in and week out. You now have the opportunity to raise the level of your consciousness through the dedication to God's word and the power of your faith in the use of His word. Let her touch your life. God sent her to teach us. Let her! Your life will never be the same. It will be so-o-o-o much better! She is a teacher extraordinary in better living.

DELLA REESE

An Open Letter to Each of You

Dear Friend:

I cannot emphasize strongly enough the importance of a change in consciousness to facilitate your healing—of whatever kind. This is the only way to guarantee a permanent change in your life. You were not created to suffer. You were not created to live a life from one malady to another.

It concerns me deeply that so many Truth students are suffering at home and in hospitals and other institutions. I know without a doubt that applying the Principle of Life will bring about wholeness and health. I know that every person, without exception, is a spiritual being. However, the demonstrations of health do not seem to be manifesting.

The Johnnie Colemon Institute (JCI) offers classes on all levels for the development of spiritual understanding. Our bookstore has one of the largest selections of New Thought literature in the city. Since our classes are full and our bookstore does very well, the only conclusion is that we are "over-read and under-done." It is impossible to change your thoughts and practice the principles without getting the results you seek.

"Practice makes permanent." Prayer and meditation must become as much a part of your daily preparation as hygiene.

God knows nothing of arthritis, diabetes, can-

cer, tuberculosis, or AIDS. Resolve this moment to pray for the elimination of these illusions from the minds of all men and women, thus eliminating them from the bodies of all human-kind.

The healing power of God did not originate with Jesus and it has not ceased with you. It is at work right now. Open your mind to the allness of God that you are. This is all that is needed to break the bonds of pain, suffering, sickness, and affliction from the life, world, and affairs of all God's children.

It works for me. It will work for you. It will work for a relative, a neighbor, a co-worker, or a stranger. Health is your birthright! Enjoy it!!!

Love,

Johnnie Colemon

Health Is Your Birthright!

It is God's will that every individual on the face of this earth should live a healthy, happy, and prosperous life. . . . Such a life is within the reach of each one of us, and the way to its attainment begins with the realizaton that the kingdom of God is within us, waiting for us to bring it into expression.

THESE ARE two of the tenets in the creed of the Universal Foundation for Better Living. Perhaps you doubt the validity of these words, because of the pain, sickness, and disease that seems to play on the center stage of your life or the life of a loved one. However, the truth is: ***Health is your birthright!***

To experience the health that is yours by divine birthright will require a change in attitude. *"If you keep doing what you're doing, you will keep getting what you're getting."* The change is in the way that you view yourself and the Universe.

For too long, too many people have believed in a punishing, judgmental, faraway God—a Deity that sent rewards and punishments on lowly "human beings." The belief is that God uses sickness, disease, and affliction to control humans and to force them to obey His commands. Some people still believe that God is always in the sky, while they live on earth. This is a sampling of the many false concepts perpetuated by a human consciousness. It has forgotten who and what it is!

Now is the time to set the record straight!

IN THE BEGINNING . . .

You are God's greatest creation. You are made in the image-likeness of God. You are a child of God. You have mastery, authority, and dominion over everything in the physical world. Your true nature is spiritual, and not human. *"You are a spiritual being, having a human experience."*

This is not a motivational speech or a spiritual pep talk, but it *is* the truth about you. This truth did not originate with me or any other minister. It originated with the One Power and One Source of all—God. It is recorded in the Bible in the first chapter of Genesis. The account of the creation is one of the most widely read and quoted passages in the Bible.

> In the beginning God created the heaven and the earth. And the earth was without form, and void; and darkness was upon the face of the deep. And the Spirit of God moved upon the face of the waters. And God said, Let there be light: and there was light. . . . And God said, Let us make

man in our image, after our likeness: and let them have dominion over the fish of the sea, and over the fowl of the air, and over the cattle, and over all the earth, and over every creeping thing that creepeth upon the earth. So God created man in his own image, in the image of God created he him; male and female created he them. And God blessed them, and God said unto them, Be fruitful and multiply, and replenish the earth and subdue it: and have dominion over the fish of the sea, and over the fowl of the air, and over every living thing that moveth upon the earth. And God said, Behold, I have given you every herb bearing seed, which is upon the face of all the earth, and every tree, in which is the fruit of a tree yielding seed; to you it shall be for meat. And to every beast of the earth, and to every fowl of the air, and to every thing that creepeth upon the earth, wherein there is life, I have given every green herb for meat: and it was so. And God saw every thing that he had made, and, behold, it was very good (Gen. 1:1–2, 26–31).

It is not written anywhere in the creation of man that his body was consumed by pain. It is not written anywhere that man, though endowed with an abundance of every good thing, would suffer with disease of no known cure, thus rendering him unable to enjoy his inheritance. But it does say, "Then God looked over all that he had made, and it was excellent in every way" (Gen. 1:31, *Living Bible*).

As a spiritual being, you may be sure: **whatever is true of God is true of you**. The nature of God is *Absolute Good*. Therefore, the nature of *you* is *Absolute Good*. God knows nothing about disease, pain, or suffering, because they are not real. Understand this: you can have mastery, authority, and dominion only over those objects that are subordinate to your nature. Undesirable situations, circumstances, and disease are not *Absolute Good*. They are illusions. The false realm of illusions is subservient to the realm of Spirit.

The notion that you are a weak, frail, dependent, and helpless human being is nothing more than an apparition. Unfortunately, this kind of erroneous belief is transferred from generation to generation as a way of man controlling man. *Nothing outside of you has any control over you!*

You are not a puppet on a string being manipulated by a bevy of puppeteers. There is no need for you to succumb to the domination of the puppeteers! Puppeteers such as heredity, peers, family, community, culture, ethnicity, socioeconomic status, society, or "fate" are not your source. These are illusions of human consciousness. Remember: *You are a spiritual being!*

The physical challenges and appearances that seem to plague your life day after day, year after year, are the layers of false beliefs and concepts that are shielding the light of your true nature. You have tolerated this kind of false domination for so long that you are convinced it is real. You have come to believe that this kind of albatross is a part of a "normal" life and will remain around your neck forever. It is not any consolation to say, "You've got to die of *something*. If you don't get *this*, you'll get *that*."

What is essential is that you get a clear understanding of *who* and *what* you are—and *Who* and *What* God is. *You must know what your relationship to God is: Father-Child (Daughter or Son).*

GOD IS LIFE, AND SO ARE YOU

One day, in the early 1950s, I received a call from my family doctor. It was one of the most unforgettable days of my life. "Johnnie," the doctor soberly said, "I can no longer be of help to you. There is no cure for your condition. Based on the diagnosis that I shared with you, the prognosis is that you have approximately six months to live." The words "six months to live" rang in my ear like the vibrations of bells ringing from a church belfry.

My mind began to race with thoughts of hurt, guilt, and fear. What did he mean that he could no longer help me? Did he not know that my whole life was ahead of me?

How could my doctor, in whom I had placed so much trust, desert me at a time like this? I had seen the many diplomas and certificates on his office wall. I knew that somewhere, someone had an explanation regarding my conditon. Why had he just given up?

I did not know what to do. However, I *did* know that I was not ready to die. Every hour seemed like a day with no hope or help in sight. I could not get the words of the conversation out of my mind. I felt betrayed by the medical profession. I wondered what I had done to deserve this.

One morning as I was sitting in the living room, still hoping that my conversation with the doctor was only a bad dream, a little book fell off the cocktail table onto the floor. This booklet was no stranger to the household, only a stranger to me. Every month my mother received one and would place it so I would surely see it. However, each time I would choose to ignore it.

As I aimlessly bent over to pick it up, eight words caught my attention: *God is your health; you can't be sick!* Those words projected a scenario so contrary to my present experience,

I felt as though an earthquake had just occurred. I wanted to know who the people were who had the nerve to print such nonsense! There I was at the point of death, as well as the countless others suffering from incurable diseases.

My mother immediately seized the opportunity to help me find these people. I feel that she was delighted because I had become open and receptive to this new religious thinking. She soon realized that I was more curious than anything else. With only six months to live, what did I have to lose? Plenty, I found out later!

Despite my formal education, I was ignorant of the kind of stuff that I was made of. I began a journey to find out how and why anyone could make such statements without any proof. Instead, I uncovered an aspect of me that I did not know existed.

The "people" I was looking for were the Unity School of Practical Christianity, at Lee's Summit, Missouri. There I journeyed, and there I gained the knowledge that gave me a new lease on life. I learned of the law of creation and that it works for me *every* time, *on* time. My only task was to apply it to my daily life.

Good health is possible because one of the attributes of God is *Life.* Life is the idea in the Mind of God of activity (animation, zest, vibrancy). Life manifests in us as health, wholeness, and energy.

✓thru us

Health is demonstrated in your experience as fitness, strength, vigor, vitality, and well-being. The opposite of health is sickness. When wholeness is evidenced in your experience, you are intact, sound, well, complete, and solid. When it is not, you appear as its opposite—diseased. Energy expresses in you as strength, potency, power, and vigor. Its opposite is weakness.

The Life Principle resides in our soul, ready, willing, and able to respond to our command. But it cannot force itself upon us: *we must activate its potential.* Life is Spirit, or the Breath of God. It unfolds in and through every fiber, cell, organ, gland, tissue, muscle, and atom

my (noticeable ✓ to others)? my call to Maureen

of our body as a witness to the Life Principle within us.

No doubt you know of a seemingly countless number of people who are in bondage to illness, pain, and disease. However, "You shall know the truth, and the truth shall set you free." Become open to the awareness of the truth that your body is the temple of the living God. It is mighty to heal and to bless you. This God-life within you is perfect. Whenever a healing need arises, you need only to call forth that Principle of Life. It will immediately respond to restore your body temple to its divine state of health.

In his book *Discover the Power within You*, Eric Butterworth writes:

> There is that of you that is greater than your weakness, stronger than your fears, the four-dimensional creature that is whole even within your sickness. This is that of you that is the perfect idea in the Mind of God. You are simply asleep to this greater self, your innate divinity. Paul says, "Awake thou that sleepest that Christ may shine upon thee" (Eph. 5:14). And what is

Christ but your own divinity, the particulariza-
tion of the Infinite source of life into the pattern
of finite embodiment. It is a perfect pattern. It is
whole. And it is you at the point of God.*

Perhaps you are wondering why some people
are well and others are not. It would be impossible for anyone to be healed of anything if
wholeness and health were not based on a principle. A principle is a basic or fundamental
truth—"the underlying plan by which Spirit
(God) moves in expressing Itself." It works the
same for you as it does for me. The choice to activate the Life Principle is made by changing
your thoughts.

Open your eyes. Remove the barriers of fear
from your soul consciousness. Affirm: *I and the
Father are One. The Principle of Life radiates
health, wholeness, energy, and vitality throughout my body temple. I am healed! Praise God,
I am healed! I am! I am! I am!*

*Eric Butterworth, *Discover the Power within You* (San
Francisco: HarperSanFrancisco, 1989), p. 165.

THE HEALING MINISTRY OF JESUS

> And a vast crowd brought him their lame, blind, maimed, and those who couldn't speak, and many others, and laid them before Jesus, and he healed them all. What a spectacle it was! Those who hadn't been able to say a word before were talking excitedly, and those with missing arms and legs had new ones; the crippled were walking and jumping around, and those who had been blind were gazing about them! (Matt. 15:31, Living Bible).

The Bible records twenty-seven specific healings performed by Jesus in addition to numerous general accounts. How could a man from Nazareth perform such feats? It was common knowledge that nothing good came out of Nazareth. This man with questionable conditions surrounding his birth—*what manner of man is this?* Eric Butterworth says that *we live in a universe that is governed by Law.* This Law is immutable and will respond to whoever makes the command. On Jesus' ministry he writes:

Jesus was not a magician. In his ministry, He simply fulfilled divine law on a higher level than anyone has before or since. The "miracle" healings were not only an evidence of the divinity of Jesus, they also evidenced the Divinity of Man— of the very person healed. The potential for healing is in every person simply because he is innately divine, innately whole and complete. Jesus' insight was so great, and He saw the divinity in the other person with such intensity, that there was a healing light. His faith quickened the sleeping potential and it sprang forth in full and perfect life.*

Every encounter is Spiritual

One-third of Jesus' ministry was devoted to healing. He taught that the Kingdom of God is within. He knew that every encounter was a spiritual encounter. Therefore, he walked among "the just and the unjust." Jesus traveled widely, teaching people the greatest secret of the ages: *"Christ in you, your hope of Glory."* Tremendous crowds followed him, because he connected with their indwelling Christ. He did not talk above their heads or command them to worship him. He informed them that they were

*Butterworth, *Discover the Power within You*, p. 161.

fully equipped to be what they wanted to be, to do what they wanted to do, and to go where they wanted to go. He further emphasized that it was not necessary to meet any criteria regarding educational or economic status. It did not matter who you were, where you had been, or where you were going. Your family background was of no significance. There was no distinction of gender, race, class, culture, or religious persuasion.

Jesus did not make a <u>determination of how far</u> <u>the affliction had advanced.</u> He did not tell the person his or her circumstance was hopeless or incurable. He never considered the length of time that the illness had occupied the body. Jesus did not inquire into the family medical history of the person seeking the healing. Jesus called forth life, health, wholeness, and perfection manifested in the individual.

Once, when Jesus was coming down a mountain, a leper approached him. He said that he knew Jesus could heal him if he wanted to. Jesus replied, "I want to." Jesus looked beyond the appearance of the condition to behold the perfection that lived within the soul of the person.

Jesus demonstrated through his many healing ''miracles'' that the Life Principle inherent in every person does not recognize anything within the individual but perfection. It toils continuously to restore the individual to his or her natural state.

Jesus encountered opposition from the Old Guard, or the intellectuals, of his day. The intellectuals believed that Jesus came to destroy the law given in the Old Testament. They were the controllers of the people, who sought them out when they were in need of healing.

Jesus emphasized to them that his mission was to fulfill the law. He was eager to share the good news that we are made in the image-likeness of God; that the Kingdom of God is within; and that every one of us is fully equipped with an abundance of every good thing.

Do you really understand the significance of the healing miracles of Jesus? Do you believe those miracles were for Jesus' time only? *Now* is the time for you to know that the healing power of God is as real today as it was in the time of Jesus. It can only happen *to* you if it can happen *through* you.

FACE THE FACTS WITH THE TRUTH

I do *not* teach that you should not go to the doctor, take medication, or spend time in the hospital. The necessity for any of these is in direct proportion to a longing to eliminate pain and suffering from the body. Good judgment and wisdom are gifts from God, and they should be exercised in all areas of your life, world, and affairs—always. To suffer or to cause another to suffer because you are "waiting on the Lord" is a misunderstanding of *Who* and *What* God is. It is also a foolish act.

I *do* teach and earnestly believe that within every person is *the whole Spirit of God*—an immutable, impersonal, unchanging, intelligent Law of Life that can restore the body to its rightful state of health. This Law, when activated by you, will without fail remove the barriers of pain, sickness, and affliction from your soul consciousness. The perfection of God will shine brightly in your body temple, because you have become open and receptive to its presence.

The instructions that are given to you by the doctors should be heeded. If you receive medication, by all means take it as directed. Bear in mind that hospitals, doctors, surgeons, and medical scientists only provide *a temporary environment* in which to *comfort* you. The *healing* takes place *within* you. Medical science *treats* diseases; it cannot *heal* you. ***Only God can heal!***

When you acknowledge the healing activity of God within, you align your mind with God-life. This promotes harmony and order throughout your body temple.

You must believe that God's vitalizing, harmonizing Life is flowing freely throughout your body every moment, recharging every part. This healing Life of God can heal what people call "incurable" as easily as it can heal a minor cut or an abrasion.

One of the lessons in *A Course in Miracles* is: "There is no order of difficulty in the universe." God knows nothing of the existence of pain, suffering, and sickness. Therefore, there is no need to classify these as fair, critical, or life-threatening. The Life Principle is based on an immutable Law of Perfection and Wholeness.

Early in my ministry, a teenager in our youth group sustained a burn on his leg from an electric blanket. Realizing the extent of the injury, his parents took him to a doctor. The doctor diagnosed the injury as a third-degree burn.

The burn covered an area the size of a silver dollar but was deeper than originally diagnosed. The parents were told that a skin graft was necessary to facilitate healing and prevent severe scarring. They agreed to the grafting procedure.

A few days after the surgery, the youth returned to the doctor. Upon evaluation, the doctor told the parents their son would receive outpatient treatment. The daily treatment was to ensure that infection was absent from the burn as well as from the wound resulting from the graft.

The treatment was painful because it consisted of a complete bandage change each time. At the end of a month, the doctor reported that the wounds were not healing and that the area had become badly infected. Moreover, if the infection persisted, amputation might be necessary.

The parents, both members of my church, called to explain the situation to me. When I arrived at the home, I told them that *it was time for immediate action*. I knew—and know—that God is as instant as I am.

I asked the parents to leave me alone with their son. They did. I asked the young man if he believed that God could heal him. He replied, "Yes." I placed my hands on both wounds and moved my hands as the Spirit directed me to do.

I spoke the word, in the name of Jesus, for life to manifest in every cell, organ, and fiber of the infected area. The young man began to tremble all over. The infected areas felt hot to the touch. I told him to thank God for his healing every time he thought about the injury.

give THANKS

The following Monday, he returned to the doctor for an evaluation for possible amputation. The doctor asked the mother what had she done in the past few days: *both of the infections were healing.* She winked at her son and told the doctor, "We prayed." The doctor told her that her prayers had miracle-working power. *They* had accomplished in *two days* what *he* was unable to do in a *month.*

Within a few weeks, the child was completely healed. He is now an adult with adult children. He and his family are active members of my church.

The medical profession has been unable to explain away the numerous cases of persons that have been completely healed when the prognosis was deemed fatal. Doctors tell me that the term used to describe these occurrences is "spontaneous remission." *My* response is that it is *God at work.* ***Only God can heal!!!***

Doctors arrive at certain conclusions based on their findings as learned in their many years of intellectual study and training. And rightly so. When I speak of "man," I am referring to man as Spirit. "Man" as the essence of God is wiser, more powerful, and more competent than his "humanness" portrays. Man's "humanness" can be measured only in years—whereas the Christ Presence, or God in us, is timeless, ageless, and universal. "Things of spirit can only be spiritually discerned."

It is documented that people are more adversely affected by the knowledge or diagnosis of a condition or disease than by the disease itself. Two of the most commonly used words by doctors when discussing illness with a patient are *diag-*

nosis and *prognosis*. There is no reason for you to allow anything to disturb the calm peace of your soul. Remember the jingle that children use: "Sticks and stones may break my bones, but words will never hurt me."

Let us take a moment and closely examine the words *diagnosis* and *prognosis*. *Diagnosis* is defined as "the process of identifying or determining the nature of a disease through examination." *Prognosis* is defined as "a prediction of the probable course and outcome of a disease; the likelihood of recovery from disease; a forecast, or a prediction."

Thus, a diagnosis is based on a set of facts supported by the doctor's training, knowledge and interpretation of the data received from laboratories, X-rays, and other instruments. Once the doctor gathers all the facts together, he theorizes and determines the plausibility of a certain progression or regression of a condition if . . .

In the definition of the word *prognosis* is the word *probable*, which means "relatively likely but not certain.'' You fall apart the moment a physician mentions cancer, AIDS, diabetes, or whatever, when the doctor is not 100 percent confident of the outcome. It is the job and profession of the physician to report these findings to you. However, as a spiritual being, you are to look within to your indwelling Christ and know that *there is nothing impossible for God*. Consequently, nothing is impossible for you.

When you fully immerse yourself into knowing, understanding, and applying the Principle of Life, you will set your soul free from the world of effects. At that moment, you will view a diagnosis as an opportunity to exercise your divinity. Because you are a spiritual being, the prognosis can only be perfection, health, and wholeness. That is the nature of the Life Principle resident within you.

Deepak Chopra, M.D., tells a story in his essay on "The Spell of Mortality":

> A middle-aged woman came to me about ten years ago complaining of severe abdominal pains

and jaundice. Believing that she was suffering from gallstones, I had her admitted for surgery. When she was opened up, it was found that she had no gallstones but a large malignant tumor that had spread to her liver, with scattered pockets of cancer throughout the abdominal cavity.

Judging the case inoperable, her surgeons closed the incision without taking any further action. Because the woman's daughter pleaded with me not to tell her mother the truth, I informed my patient that the gallstones had been removed successfullly. I rationalized that her family would break the news to her in time, and that at best she had only a few months to live— at least she could spend them with peace of mind.

Eight months later I was astonished to see the woman in my office. She had returned for a routine physical exam, which revealed no jaundice, pain or detectable signs of cancer. Only a year later did she confess anything unusual to me. She said, "Doctor, I was so sure I had cancer then that when it turned out to be just gallstones, I told myself I would never be sick another day in my life." Her cancer never recurred.

This case has led me to consider that modern medicine has restricted itself to an extremely narrow view of healing. The question we should ask is not "What is healing?" It has always been known that healing is a process controlled by nature. The crucial question is, rather, "Does healing have any natural limit?" So far as I know, the answer is no.*

"Healing is not a process, it is a revelation. . . . Perfect God, Perfect Man, Perfect Being."† You need not fully understand the *how, what,* and *why* of healing to be healed. Stand firm in your conviction that *you are all that God is.* Do not allow yourself to give up when the appearance or condition shows signs of regression. Become like Jacob, and wrestle with the angel (Principle of Life within you) until it blesses you.

THANK you God for the blessing this situation has for me!

*From *Healers on Healing*, Richard Carlson and Benjamin Shield, eds. (New York: G. P. Putnam's Sons, A Jeremy Tarcher/Putnam Book, 1989), pp. 179, 180.
†Ernest Holmes.

The Faith Factor

THE STORY is told of a doctor who had a lawyer for a patient. The lawyer was plagued with migraine headaches. The doctor prescribed some small pills to be kept at all times in his breast pocket. Whenever the lawyer felt an oncoming attack, he would take one of the little pills. Immediately, his pain would dissipate.

One day the lawyer was involved in a very notable case. He had to be focused, placid, and alert. At the beginning of the trial, of all times, he felt a headache coming on. He knew that he could not afford a delay of any kind. As usual, he reached into his pocket, got his pill, and swallowed it. Like clockwork, the pain vanished.

Later in the day, he returned to his office. As he was examining some documents, he discovered a mistake on one of them. The mistake just needed to be erased and all would be fine. He always kept the small eraser end of a pencil in his pocket for incidents such as this.

Much to his surprise, when he reached into his pocket the eraser was not there, but the little pill was. He had swallowed the eraser! And the eraser had worked as well as the little pill had.

Why? He believed that the pill would stop his headache pain. Because he believed without a doubt that it would work, it did. It was not the pill or the eraser that facilitated the remedy. It was the faith that he placed in either thing that did the work!

WHAT IS FAITH?

Faith is "the perceiving power of the mind linked with the power to shape substance. . . . the power to do the seemingly impossible" (Charles Fillmore). Faith is "absolute certainty." Faith is "trust without reservation." "Faith is the substance of things hoped for, the evidence of things not seen" (Heb. 11:1, KJV). "It is the confident assurance that something we want is going to happen. It is the certainty that what we hope for is waiting for us, even though we cannot see it up ahead" (Heb. 11:1, Living Bible). Faith is the power to *focus* on God the Good.

The healing that you are seeking is ready and waiting for you. To exercise your faith means to direct your attention to God. You are impregnated with health, wholeness, and energy. Faith is the "go power" in you: the Life Principle waits patiently for you to rev it up with faith.

Exercise your faith!

Faith is to an *idea* what *soil* is to a *seed*. Faith

is an idea in Divine Mind embodying hope, trust, belief, and expectancy.

FAITH SEES! Faith perceives the possibility of the result long before there is any visible sign. Faith is the ability in you to see the condition healed regardless of what is being manifested. Faith is your spiritual eye. It looks within and perceives the good in the midst of the appearance.

FAITH KNOWS! Faith is more than idle hoping or believing. Faith knows the truth that God's outpouring of Himself is irrepressible, infinite, and absolute. When you are consciously aware of this, your faith grows courageously and trusts God to get the best out of the worst.

Faith is your spiritual fingers. It reaches into the spiritual realm and lifts your eyes above all material things and points to the spirit as the source of all. "I will lift up mine eyes unto the hills, from whence cometh my help. My help cometh from the Lord, which made heaven and earth" (Ps. 121:1, 2).

FAITH GROWS! As your faith grows, your mental images change from bondage to liberty, from darkness to light, from sickness to health, and from poverty to abundance. The more faith we practice, the more faith we have. *Use is the law of increase.* Understand: faith is not something you *have* or *do not have.* The choice is only to *use* it or not.

Practice faith

use it or NOT!

"When in doubt, faith is out!"

"MOUNTAIN, BE THOU REMOVED"

> If you only have faith in God—this is the absolute truth—you can say to this Mount of Olives, "Rise up and fall into the Mediterranean," and your command will be obeyed. All that's required is that you really believe and have no doubt! Listen to me! You can pray for *anything*, and *if you believe, you have it*; it's yours! (Mark 11:22–24, Living Bible).

Poor health is a mountain that has too many of us believing that it cannot be removed. Every person is created spritually perfect. The seeming imperfections and appearances are not reality. Under your physical body is the real of you: perfect, whole, and complete. You express in your body what you believe.

If you do not believe that health and wholeness are yours for the asking, they will not happen to you. If you do not believe that a paper cut can be healed, it will not heal for you. God's will is not for you to be sick or unhealthy. However, if you persist in your belief that sickness is a reality in your life, then it must be. *It is the law.*

In the 1970s, I had the pleasure of meeting Della Reese, star of stage and film. I always admired her for her talents and gifts in the show-business world. Shortly after our meeting, Della had a physical challenge.

One day while taping the *Tonight Show*, she collapsed and was rushed to the hospital. The doctors diagnosed her case as an aneurysm of the brain. Based on the test results, they felt that the prognosis was not good.

Della being a Truth student at the time, she wanted them to tell her everything. The doctors explained to her that 93 percent of all cases like this were fatal. Della said, "I do not want to talk or hear about them. Please tell me about the 7 percent of survivors: *that* is the group I choose!"

The doctors insisted that she needed to be realistic and understand the full scope of the situation. She told them that she *was* being realistic and that *she* was in the 7 percent group. If they were not the physicians who administer to that group, could they please direct her to the appropriate ones!

Della and I prayed and agreed that what was essential to facilitate her complete healing was being ready, willing, and able to go to work. *"It works if you work it!"* The instrument that the doctors needed became available at the exact time of the operation. "God is!"

On the way to the operating room, Della joyfully sang her favorite song, "God Is So Wonderful.'' The medical team had already told Della the post-operative side-effects to expect. Her eyesight might not be restored for a couple of days. Della kept her vigil of *"God is; I am!"*

I received a call on a Sunday morning from the hospital; it was not the doctor or Della's husband, Franklin, or her son. It was Miss Della. She said. ''Buddy, God has done it again.'' I said, ''What are you doing on the phone? Remember, you must use wisdom.''

She said, ''I *am* using it. I wanted to call to let you know that the doctors are baffled. Bless their hearts. I'm not supposed to be able to see for a while. However, I can see everything in this room! Praise God!!!'' She went on to describe everything in the room in full detail.

I was floating on Cloud Nine when I arrived at church that morning. We were celebrating our Twenty-third Church Anniversary, we had a guest speaker, and I had planned to take somewhat of a subordinate role in the service. However, God had other plans.

THY FAITH HATH MADE THEE WHOLE

As I was about to leave the chapel at the close of the second service, a young woman walked up to me and started to cry. Falling into my arms, she told me that she and her husband had planned to come to the first service, but his physical condition prevented them from doing so. Seven days earlier he had injured his back while shoveling snow.

What started as a little discomfort had grown progressively worse to the point that he could not stand up. He had been to the emergency room of a hospital the previous day. The physician on duty prescribed some pain-relievers and muscle-relaxers. She did not admit him because she wanted him to see a certain orthopedic surgeon on Monday.

The husband, Mr. M, was parking the car. Mrs. M said that he was 6′2″ tall and was bent over from the waist. The only way that he could escape the excruciating pain was to get on his hands and knees, like an animal. All night they had listened to tapes of the various church services to receive a healing.

She felt that if they could only get to church, her husband could be healed. She had previous experience with spiritual healing and had faith in God's healing power. Mr. M was in so much pain he was open to anything. The medication had not helped at all.

I instructed her to take a seat and I would come to them sometime during the service. I had no idea what I was going to do; but I knew that *something* was happening, because the power of the Holy Spirit was all over me.

This young couple drove seventeen miles in the cold and snow because they had faith in God as a healer. They had not been deterred by the delay in getting dressed due to the husband's condition. They were determined to push through the crowd and touch the hem of His garment for health!

I wondered that with all the people we have on

Sunday, especially at the third service, how would I find them? But God had taken care of that. They were sitting in the seats next to my mother. I was led by God to talk of my conversation with Della. I told of her just staring at everything in that hospital room, because she knew that *faith sees*. Then I told the congregation about a young woman and her husband who had wanted to attend the first service but could not. The husband had a challenge in his back that made him unable to stand up straight.

I asked the congregation to close their eyes, join hands, and focus all thoughts on God. I emphasized the power of a collective consciousness. Furthermore, it was essential to know without a doubt that *"Health is your birthright."*

I stepped from the platform and went to the couple's row. I prayed with Mr. M for a few moments before God instructed me to get him out of the seat and into the aisle. When he moved into the aisle, he was bent over and obviously in pain. God directed my hands to the small of his back and then up and down his left leg. Each time he would stand a little straighter. Finally, I told him to put his hands over his head. There he was, standing 6'2'' tall, hands extended high above his head and tears rolling down his cheeks. He was repeating the words, ''Thank you God!'' over and over.

I told him to walk back and forth, bend over and up repeatedly, and he did. Between his tears he told me that he had no pain for the first time in seven days. He had been unable to sleep in his bed or get any rest at all.

Meanwhile, Mrs. M had been under the power of the Holy Spirit from the beginning of the healing service. She did not see any of this take place. When she was helped off the floor and became conscious, all she could see was her husband, standing tall, thanking and praising God. And out she went again!

Mr. M had not believed healing was possible in this manner. He had gone along with his wife because she was so convinced, and he felt he had nothing to lose. If nothing else, he always enjoyed the service. He confessed that when I touched his back and his leg, something extremely hot left that area and took the pain with it. He described it as a large hot coal that walked out of his body—like a special-effects demonstration in a television show.

The next morning his pain returned. He wanted to know what he had done to prevent the sustaining of the healing. They decided to take the advice of the emergency room physician and see the doctor that she had recommended. When they arrived at the doctor's office, he was furious that any physician would allow a patient to leave the hospital in the state that Mr. M was in. He called the other doctor and gave her a piece of his mind.

He immediately admitted Mr. M to the hospital and began to run a battery of tests. From the begining, Mr. M told the doctor that he would not agree to an operation. All his friends, relatives, and co-workers had told him tragic stories about people they knew who had operations on the back. So he was determined that he would not go "under the knife."

The next Sunday Mrs. M came to me to explain, sadly, that Mr. M had not sustained the healing. He was in the hospital. I explained to her that *he was already healed*. The hospital experience was necessary because he had to work something out in his soul consciousness. I appealed to her to see him as God sees him: perfect, whole, and complete—also, to keep that image of him standing in front of the chapel, hands extended, thanking and praising God. She said that she would.

The therapy and other treatments did not improve his condition. The only choice left was an operation. The husband stood firm and said absolutely not. Meanwhile, the wife had read about a procedure to remedy the situation without an operation. The procedure was innovative and was not approved for execution in the United States. The doctor discussed the procedure with them and said that he would make the necessary arrangements if this was what they wanted.

However, the doctor felt that time was running

out and knew that he could help Mr. M through a successful operation. He said, ''I do not know if it is my ego or what. But I know that I can help you if you will give me a chance.'' As the couple was leaving his office, he told them to consider the operation rather than go out of the country for an expensive, virtually untried procedure.

On the way home they talked about faith. If they believed that God is the healer, could they not trust Him to guide the doctor during the operation? By the time they arrived home, the decision was made: to have faith in God and agree to the operation. Also, to tell only three people about the operation: their best friend; Johnnie Colemon; and the wife's grandmother.

AGREE to Surgery [handwritten margin note]

They arrived home so late that they felt the doctor was no longer in the office. They decided to call anyway and leave a message with his answering service. To their amazement, the doctor answered by saying, ''Mr. and Mrs. M, I *knew* you would call. I know that you have agreed to have the operation. I was prepared to stay here all night if I had to. Do not be afraid. God and I always work as a team.''

The doctor was very excited about the operation. When Mrs. M arrived at the hospital, the operation had been over for hours. Mr. M was out of recovery and the doctor had gone to his office. When she called him, he said, ''The operation only took one-fourth of the time we originally estimated. When we opened him up, it was not at all what we thought. It was a very minor procedure. You will wonder if I operated at all. The scar will be virtually nonexistent.''

Mr. M wanted to know if he would need to take therapy. The naysayers had found out about the operation and had started their post-operative commentary. The doctor said, ''If you *want* to go to therapy, you may do so. There is no need. Everything medically possible has been done. *You must heal from within!*''

Mr. M was back to work, 100 percent healed, in less than a month!

FAITH THAT CONQUERS

As I mentioned in my "Open Letter" to you (see p. xi), it is a matter of deep concern to me that so many Truth students are experiencing pain, disease, and affliction. I know—and know that I know—that ***God is a healer!*** The only action that you need to take is to *"have faith in God."* Faith is your ability to say "Yes" to God. It sounds simple enough. However, something is wrong!

Do you feel that faith is something that you need to *get*? Are you *afraid* of something? Do you think that your condition is *hopeless*? Do you wonder how much *work* is required to activate faith? Do you feel that you are not *worthy*? What is the problem?

You have all the faith that you will ever have. And so do I. When you are centered in faith, fear disappears. When you understand the power of faith, you will know there is nothing too hard for God. And there is nothing too hard for you.

we have ALL THE FAITH WE NEED!

[handwritten: What are the benefits of the condition]

Too often you are willing to remain in pain, rather than "pick up your bed and walk." You need not worry about stumbling as you move out on faith. You are not walking alone! Affirm: ***"God and I are One!"*** Repeat this affirmation over and over until you feel the shackles of doubt, fear and cynicism leave your soul consciousness.

Jesus emphasized that there is no reason or excuse for you to be burdened with poor health. He said that living the life you were created to live does not require you to run an obstacle course. Jesus worked hard at trying to get you to understand that your faith center is HIGH VOLTAGE! It only takes a small amount equal to the size of a mustard seed to move any mountain of pain, sickness, or disease from your body. This "itty-bitty" measure of faith is capable of opening blind eyes, raising the dead, restoring mobility to the lame, and healing every kind of illness plaguing humankind.

Read for yourself the story of the woman afflicted with an issue of blood for twelve years.

You will find the story in Matthew 9:20–22. Jesus was on his way to the home of a Jewish leader. The leader's daughter was dead and he wanted Jesus to come to his home and restore her back to life. As always, a throng of people followed wherever Jesus traveled. For you see, they thought they were following a man. However, what had happened was that the Christ within them had been awakened.

As they were walking, a woman who had been hemorrhaging for over twelve years followed the crowd. It is written that when you are ready for a healing, the healer appears. This day she decided that she could be healed. She understood that with the number of people who needed ministering to, the chances of her having a private audience with Jesus were remote. But I believe that her faith center was on fire, and it urged her to "go for it"—for that is its duty. The realization that all you need is a "mustard seed" of contact to be healed had permeated her entire being. She felt that all she needed to do was "touch the hem of His garment" and be made whole.

That fire of faith within her provided the impetus to push through the fears, doubts, disappointments, pain, and suffering and make contact with the Great Physician. The vibration of her faith was intense. Jesus felt it and wanted to know, "Who touched me?" Regardless of what is going on around you, when the Holy Spirit has been illumined within you, you feel something different. I always say, "If you don't feel nothing, you don't have nothing!"

What do you need to do to light the fire of faith within you? To be sure, I don't feel that the same technique works for everybody. *I* like to listen to music. Music has always been the catalyst to assist me in focusing on the power of faith within me.

The Temple Ensemble sings a song entitled "Faith That Conquers." The words are a series of affirmative statements of faith. If you do not sing very well, that is okay. Understand that the word *conquer* means "to overcome." If you do not have a recording of the song, just meditate on the words:

I have the FAITH that
Sees the invisible,
Receives the impossible;
Faith that can conquer anything.

FAITH that uproots my problems.
FAITH to know that God can solve them.
FAITH to vision my freedom.
I have the FAITH that can conquer anything.

FAITH that uproots your problems.
FAITH to know that God can solve them.
FAITH to vision your freedom.

I have the FAITH that can conquer anything.

FAITH
To reach the unreachable.
FAITH
To fight the unbeatable.
FAITH
To see the invisible.

I have the FAITH that can conquer anything.

These are powerful words! You must choose to allow the words to become real inside of you. You are an overcomer because *you are faith!* Your *faith* is the anchor that keeps you steady while the seas of pain and ill-health are raging.

Through the power of FAITH, Noah built the ark.

Through the power of FAITH, Abraham left the land of his birth.

Through the power of FAITH, Abraham offered Isaac.

Through the power of FAITH, Jochebed hid the baby Moses.

Through the power of FAITH, Jericho's wall came tumbling down.

Through the power of FAITH, David over-powered Goliath.

Through the power of FAITH, the widow of Zarephath fed Elijah.

Through the power of FAITH, Joseph fled to Egypt.

And,

Through the power of FAITH, *You are making your overcoming now!*

CHAPTER 3

The Thought Connection

WHEN I entered the gates of the Unity School of Practical Christianity, I knew I would not return the same way that I entered. I was on a mission. A mission with a far deeper purpose than I had even imagined. Little did I know that before I talked to God about my health concern, He had already answered my prayers.

The founders of Unity School, Charles and

Myrtle Fillmore, had demonstrated in their own lives the power of God as healer. One of Charles Fillmore's legs was shorter than the other. He learned that God is Life. Through the application of universal laws, the shorter leg grew to the length of the longer. His wife, Myrtle, was healed of an incurable disease. I was journeying in the right direction! The people at Unity had learned the Law, understood the Law, and applied the Law.

My doctor did not know how right he was when he said to me, "Johnnie, you have six months to live." As I reflect on that memorable conversation, he was absolutely right. I want to take the time to thank him. Wherever you are, Mr. Doctor, I thank and praise God for you.

You see, I had only "six months to live" in that old way of *thinking* about who I am, Who God is, and my relationship to God. In one of my first classes, the instructor dropped a bombshell: *"You are the thinker that thinks the thought that makes the thing."* Thoughts of doom, negativity, jealousy, victimization, and unworthiness were the root causes of disease. Thus, disease was caused by wrong thoughts, beliefs, and opinions. *Wow!!!*

Indeed, I had to ponder those statements. If this instructor was right, *my* thinking was responsible for *my* physical condition. Maybe the doctor's prognosis was a little off: he might have given me too much time! I had to get to work on me immediately!

I admonish you not to wait until some doctor tells you that you have only "six months to live" to get sincere. Get back on track to your natural state of health *now*. If the doctor has already articulated this message, it is time for you to go to work.

Stop for a moment. Repeat the following words ten times silently: ***I am the thinker that thinks the thought that makes the thing.*** Did you get the same feeling that I did? Did you ask yourself the question, "Could *I* really be the cause of disease in my body?" If it is me that is the cause, then I need to find out what I must do.

"BE YE TRANSFORMED"

The power of thought is the highest power given to us. You can choose what to think, and what not to think. Unlike other creations, you can choose to accept direction from your indwelling Christ or to disavow your true nature. However, when you realize that thought is your connecting link to God and to the Kingdom of Heaven, you become the master that you were created to be. This mastery enables you to live a healthy, happy, and prosperous life.

Since the beginning of time, philosophers, scholars, and sages have understood the power of thought. The masses, however, do not understand their divine nature. Therefore, generation after generation continues to view itself as "merely human."

Consequently, we fall prey, without fail, to the illusions of disease, pain, and affliction associated with the human condition.

Most of us feel that we have a mind of our own.

This could not be further from the truth. There is only one mind, the Mind of God. Charles Fillmore states it this way:

> We have NO independent mind; there is only universal Mind, but we have consciousness in that mind and we have control over that consciousness. We have control over our own thoughts, and our thoughts make up our consciousness.

You are three-fold in nature: Spirit, Soul, Body. The Soul of you is your mind or consciousness. Your mind has a threefold structure: superconscious mind, or Christ mind; conscious mind, or intellect; and the subconscious mind, or creative mind.

Jesus discovered his divine nature. He attained the Christhood. When we refer to Jesus as our Wayshower, we are speaking of Jesus the Christ and not Jesus the man. Jesus' thoughts were rooted in the superconscious phase of mind. He did not judge according to what his five senses presented to him. His intellect or conscious phase of mind was spiritualized. Therefore, he saw everything as it truly was, an expression of God. His ability to perform miraculous healings and other miracles was the perfect outworking of the Law. The subconscious mind of Jesus was filled with love, peace, joy, and every good thing. There was nothing to demonstrate but the allness of God.

I have always maintained the opinion that "if we knew better, we would do better." There is no way that anyone of sound mind would suffer needlessly if she knew of a sure way out of a situation. Do you agree?

Your day-to-day interactions are accomplished through the conscious state of mind. In this phase you choose, reason, judge, accept, or reject thoughts, opinions, and beliefs. The conscious is influenced by family, society, trends, public opinions, heredity, and the race consciousness.

Understand that Jesus lived from the superconscious phase of mind. Your aim is to abide in the

Christ Mind. Human conditioning is the root of this shift away from your divine nature. However, like the prodigal son, you are in a regeneration stage, returning your thoughts to their proper place, the Christ Mind.

This regeneration is accomplished through the use of affirmations and denials as a means to cleanse the entire consciousness. Then the Holy Spirit has a clear path to express through. This process is an *inner* toil, and you can do your mental work in any kind of physical environment. However, your inner self must be still, relaxed, and calm.

"EVERY THOUGHT IS A PRAYER"

You know that you have no mind of your own. However, you have consciousness *in the One Mind*, and you have *control* over your consciousness. Consciousness is the essence or totality of attitudes, opinions, and sensitivities held, or thought to be held, by an individual.

Consciousness is awareness. You cannot have anything that you are not aware of.

After the shock of finding out that my thoughts shaped my life, I learned that ***"There is nothing to be healed, only God to be revealed."*** In other words, to allow free expression of the perfect Christ mind that exists within me and within you. Because thought is your connecting link to God, it is through daily prayer and meditation that you return to your "Father's house."

By "turn within" we mean centering your thoughts on the One Power, the One Presence, the omnipotent, omnipresent, and omniscient God. With your thoughts centered on God, you can only demonstrate in your life the nature of God the Absolute Good. Often, I do not name maladies, such as cancer, arthritis, etc., because I do not want these names to become a part of my consciousness. Instead, I create a word, like *"bonkus-of-the-conkus."* ("Bonkus" is a mixture of *bunkum* and *bogus*!)

You may feel that your physical challenge is of

such magnitude that you cannot possibly focus on God. *Friend, you can!* You are God in all of His magnificence. Even when your body is in pain, "know that ye are gods." As you gain a deeper understanding of the role that thought plays in your life, controlled thinking will become a lifestyle rather than an occasional exercise.

"Every thought is a prayer." But what *kind* of prayer? It is absolutely necessary that you regain control of your thoughts. "Nature abhors a vacuum." Thoughts that are causing you unnecessary pain and agony are running and ruining your life. Put a stop to this now!

> The body is the servant of the mind. It obeys the operations of the mind, whether they be deliberately chosen or automatically expressed. . . . Disease and health, like circumstances, are rooted in thought. . . . Thoughts of fear have been known to kill a man as speedily as a bullet, and they are continually killing thousands of people just as surely though less rapidly. . . . The body . . . responds readily to the thoughts by which it is impressed, and habits of thought will

produce their own effects, good or bad, upon it. . . . Change of diet will not help a man who will not change his thoughts. When a man makes his thoughts pure, he no longer desires impure food. . . . If you would perfect your body, guard your mind. If you would renew your body, beautify your mind. Thoughts of malice, envy, disappointment, despondency, rob the body of its health and grace. . . . There is no physician like cheerful thought for dissipating the ills of the body. . . . To live continually in thoughts of ill will, cynicism, suspicion, and envy is to be confined in a self-made prison-hole. (James Allen, *As a Man Thinketh*)

You must arrange a special time each day for prayer and meditation. Prayer is communion, or *common union*, between God and yourself. You are to pray in faith, understanding, and determination. Keep in mind that you are not praying to change God, but to lift your thoughts from sickness to health. Paul said it best: "Be ye transformed by the renewing of your mind" (Romans 12:2).

"AS A MAN THINKETH"

Emerson says, "A man becomes what he thinks about all day long." The Bible states, "For as he thinketh in his heart, so is he" (Proverbs 23:7). *"What I think and believe in, I become. What I become, I attract."*

What does it mean to think? To think is to use the powers of the mind, as in conceiving ideas, drawing inferences, making judgments, using the faculty of reason, having an opinion, forming mental images, viewing in a certain way, and renewing an image or thought in the mind. Often we tell children to "put on your thinking cap," meaning to use your head.

This is all I am saying to you: use your mind for *health*, not *sickness*. Make a conscious decision to no longer sit by the pool waiting for someone to help you in (see John 5:1–9). The life forces of health, energy, and wholeness are perpetually stirred, awaiting your call. If no one in your home, on your job, or at the hospital believes in the power of thought to heal, believe and apply it for yourself. ***You and God are always a majority.***

A few years ago, the following article, "I Believe in Miracles," appeared in a leading women's magazine:

> The doctor leaned back in his padded wooden chair and tossed his pen onto the blotter. "I'm afraid there's not much more we can do for your cancer, Mrs. N," he solemnly stated. "We'll continue with the chemotherapy and radiation treatment and just hope for the best." That night, Mrs. N sat on her bed, frustrated and depressed. "What good is it?" she frowned. "Even the doctors don't have any hope!"
>
> Then, as she sat in the quiet of that crucial night, a warm feeling began to well up inside of her, like a glowing ember that refused to be extinguished. It was a sense that there was something more that could be done, something greater than chemicals and doctors and prognoses. But what?
>
> Into her mind flashed the thought of her son, Jack, who she knew had been involved for years with what he called "holistic health." Now she felt an urge to ask her son more about what he was doing.

The principles were simple: We create our lives, including health and illness, with our thoughts. To be successful and fulfillfed, we must learn to use our minds constructively, using clear, positive images as building blocks. These mind-pictures are absorbed into our subconscious which, in turn, brings our new, uplifting thoughts into reality in the form of health, abundance and peacefulness.

These principles seemed right to Mrs. N, somehow strangely familiar and comfortingly real. It was as if she already knew them, but had forgotten their truth. So Mrs. N began to practice. Every day for two sessions, one-half hour each, she would sit in a comfortable chair, relax and visualize a bright light, something like a bolt of lightning flashing into the cancerous part of her body. Then she would visualize this light breaking up the cells, shattering them into thousands of tiny pieces. Again and again and again, she practiced this picturing, until she saw her entire body as clear and whole and healthy.

Meanwhile, as the Law of Attraction would have it, Mrs. N was directed to another doctor who worked by the dynamic principles that she had discovered.

"It's very clear to me, Mrs. N," stated the doctor, "you can live and be healthy if that is what you choose. You must think positively and realize that there is a greater Healer, far more powerful than myself or any other human being. If you attune your mind to this great healing energy, it will surely work for you.''

This bright advice encouraged Mrs. N to continue even more enthusiastically with her visualization. Two weeks later, she returned to the laboratory for X-rays. After completing the tests, the doctors walked out of the darkroom shaking their heads and checking the X-rays over and over and over again.

''We don't quite know how to explain this, Mrs. N,'' reported one of the medical team, ''but your condition has improved considerably. As you can see on these X-rays, most of the cancerous cells have been broken apart, as if they have been shattered, and it looks as if they are being expelled from your system!''

Mrs. N smiled and said a quiet prayer of thanks. Then she went home to visualize some more. Within a few months, Mrs N was given a clean bill of health.*

When the scripture speaks of the heart, it is referring to your subconscious mind. The sub-

*By Alan Cohen, in John K. Williams, *The Wisdom of Your Subconscious Mind* (Prentice-Hall, 1973).

conscious does not know how to separate a joke from the truth. Its nature is to record what you think, say, and feel. Then it replays the cumulative thoughts in your life as your day-to-day experiences. I have dedicated my life to instructing people to *"watch your words," "watch your thoughts," "watch your actions," "watch your reactions,"* and to *"watch your feelings."* You are a powerhouse, and you do not realize it. This is the reason you continue to harm yourself.

CUT THE TIES THAT BIND YOU TO THE HUMAN! Through the renewing of your mind, turn back to God. *The journey to God is without distance.* Have you not wondered why you get such a great feeling in church? It is because the focus is on the goodness and grace of God. I truly wish that I could do it for you. I know how important it is for you to think only thoughts of God.

CUT THE TIES THAT BIND YOU TO HEREDITY! You are a free-will being. The choice to acknowledge your divine nature must be made by *you*. Perhaps you started to change your way of thinking but fell by the wayside. *You are the master of your life.* You may start and stop any time you desire. Oftentimes, we blame our family, work environment, or others for preventing us from staking our spiritual claim. "Greater is he that is within you than he that is in the world."

CUT THE TIES THAT BIND YOU TO CIRCUM-STANCES! Jesus told the man by the pool to "get up and go home!" He did not say, "Give your hand to me so I can help you into the waters." It was not the waters, but the faith that people had placed in them. If the waters were the Source of healing, the man would have had to get into the waters. *Your miracle cure is within you.* Become open and receptive to it. God is your Source of health. Awaken to the God idea within you. *"God is your health; you can't be sick!"*

PRAYER CHANGES THINGS

One of the principles that I learned at Unity School was to go to God first and then move as

God directs. So often when you are faced with a health challenge, your first action is to focus on the pain and the condition. In this agitated state, you tend to run to and fro, following the advertised fastest remedy. To your dismay, this scattered thought and activity is fruitless.

Prayer is a communication system between you and God. Its effectiveness is not based on the position you pray in (kneeling, standing, head bowed, eyes closed, hands clasped, or hands open). It is your right disposition that is necessary for a prayerful environment. When you pray, you must still the chatterbox in your mind.

Your prayer is an acknowledgment of the omniscience, omnipresence, and omnipotence of God. Remember to pray in secret: prayer is personal. *"Be still and know that I am God."* Still all thoughts in the outer and center all thoughts on God. *"Have faith in God."* Know that your prayer lifts you to the realization that God is all there is. Release your prayer to the Universe and give thanks for the desired results. God will direct you from this point.

During the last visit that my friend Raymond Charles Barker made to Chicago, he told a wonderful story demonstrating the power of prayer. One of his senior associate ministers slipped and fell in her home one evening. She felt and heard her hip crack. Immediately, she started to pray, giving herself a spiritual mind treatment: *"I am a perfect spiritual being. God's substance is never broken. I walk through the glory of God. God's substance is always perfect, in its right place and at the right time."* Afterward, she dialed the church's prayer ministry and notified them of the situation. She told them to "go to work" immediately—*prayer* work. She said that she was giving them only twenty minutes, after which she would call for an ambulance.

True to her word, she telephoned for the paramedics after twenty minutes. When the ambulance arrived, she was diagnosed with a broken hip. The paramedics told her that they would be careful in moving her because they realized the excruciating pain she was experiencing. She remarked that she was not in pain. They said,

"You have a broken hip." She replied, "What does that have to do with pain?"

When she arrived at the hospital, she was responsive to all of their directions and instructions. She said that wherever she is, God is, and she reacts accordingly. The operation went well. The doctor prescribed pain-relievers for her, but she did not take them, because she had no pain. When she was released from the hospital, her recovery period was far less than "normal." The doctor gave her pain-relievers to take home. When she returned to his office two months later, she did not have a cane, and she returned the full bottle of pain pills. She never experienced any pain.

The medical profession is engaged in several scientific studies to prove the effectiveness of prayer. I am happy to see that doctors are acknowledging the healing powers of prayer. Frankly, I am not surprised—because there is only One Mind.

Larry Dossey, M.D., author of *Healing Words*, is urging the medical profession to pay attention to the effects of prayer—because the results will "knock your socks off." He tells of an experiment that was conducted by San Francisco General Hospital cardiologist Dr. Randolph Byrd with 400 heart patients. Half of the patients were chosen at random to be prayed for by strangers. The other half were not prayed for. The patients, nurses, and doctors involved in the experiment did not know who was being prayed for and who was not. The strangers only knew the first names and a few details about the people they were praying for.

When the experiment was concluded, the doctor said that the results were *"striking."* The prayed-for group did significantly better than the other patients. Fewer of them died of heart attacks. Furthermore, none of them needed mechanical help to breathe. One doctor called it a "miracle." The study showed that somehow the prayer of strangers traveled across time and space. People were positively affected without knowing that others were praying for them.

Dr. Dossey says that this means that some part of the human mind is omnipresent in space, eternal in time. The Nobel Prize–winning physicists that are studying the "prayer phenomenon" are saying, "There are no boundaries around the individual mind. Then, at some point there can not be several billion minds, there can only be One Mind." Dr. Dossey says that if the world just understood the power of prayer, peace would be everywhere.

Giving thanks is the highest form of prayer. Affirm: *Father-Mother God, I thank you that you have heard me and I know you hear me always. Thanks, God, for the revitalizing, re-energizing, and recharging of every cell in my body Temple. I go forth right now renewed, refreshed, and recharged with the vigor, vitality, and alertness of God. I am the healthy, whole, and mighty child of a loving Father. I am healed! Praise God! I am healed! Thanks, God! And so it is.*

CHAPTER 4

There Is No Hiding-Place

HAVE YOU wondered how everything emerges in your life, world, and affairs as a Truth lesson? Even when you are not consciously aware of the necessity! The newspaper comic character Ziggy is a great Truth teacher. Ziggy is often philosophical and introspective. In one of his panels Ziggy is standing at the window, looking out. He says, "It's not possible to 'get away from it all' . . . 'cause everywhere I go . . . THERE I AM!'' Ziggy, you are right on target!

God is omnipresent, everywhere equally present; therefore *you* are everywhere equally present. *''There is no spot where God is not!'' ''Nothing is ever lost in Spirit.''* These are axiomatic expressions that are commonly utilized and notably misunderstood and misinterpreted by Truth students.

The divine nature of you is not hidden from you. It is always with you. It *is* you. When you are gripped by sickness, you turn every way but within. You do not want to hear any of ''that God stuff.'' But the very thing you do not want to hear is the answer to your prayer. The pain and suffering that you are experiencing or witnessing is just your body symbolizing what your mind believes. You are being blind to the powerhouse that you are.

You can never get away from who *and whose* you are. No amount of pain, disease, or affliction can hide the truth that *you are spiritual, created to be healthy, whole, and complete.* No amount of pain, disease, or affliction can hide the truth that *your thoughts determine the kind of life you will experience.* When you change the pattern of your thoughts, you change the pattern of your experiences.

I enjoy attending seminars conducted by intellectuals who have come to the realization of our divinity. When the speaker is a medical doctor, I am really overjoyed. Perhaps if you hear the truth delivered by different channels, you will start to believe it. For too long, the medical profession has denied the existence of a Higher Power. Countless studies in psychoneuroimmunology (mind/body medicine) are being conducted in universities and medical schools all over the world.

Dr. Deepak Chopra, M.D., the noted author, was exceptional—as always—in a recent seminar I attended. He destroyed some of the illusions and barriers that we hide behind. This is a small sampling of his talk:

Whatever you encounter is nothing more than you. The cells that protect you from infections are constantly eavesdropping on your dialogue. The human body is a physical machine that manufactures thoughts. People die from preventable disease. We cannot step into the same water twice, because new water is constantly flowing. The same is with our bodies; we are being renewed every second. Our physical body is recycled earth, water and air. We get a new skin once a month, a new skeleton once every three months and a new liver every five days.

This is the truth! Finally the medical profession agrees! Now, what barrier have you placed between perfect health and *you*?

WHAT DID HINDER YOU?

Moses received a commission from God at the "burning bush." He was to lead the children of Israel from the bondage of Pharaoh. Moses accepted the appointment with trepidation. Why would his people believe that the God of their fathers had sent him to accomplish such a feat? God is all there is, there is nothing else. God told

Moses "I AM THAT I AM." "Just tell them that I AM has directed you."

What Moses had learned during the burning bush experience was that "I AM" is God's name for Himself. "I AM" is the Christ Mind or spiritual identity within every person. Remember, *whatever is true of God is true of you.*

Let us analyze this for a moment. How many times have you used the words "I AM"? Probably more times than you can calculate. In what *manner* do you use the words "I AM"? Bear in mind that this is God's name. Do you use these words in positive, constructive statements? Do you not know the power that is in the name of God?

A secret of healing from biblical times is that whatever you affix to God's name, "I AM," manifests in your life. The association can be conscious, unconscious, positive, or negative. If you affirm, "I AM sick!" or "I AM inheriting this from my mother!" what do you suppose is obliged to occur?

You are an individualized expression of the One Power, One Presence, God. God loves you so much that He does not impose His will (Absolute God) upon you. Freedom to choose what you want to say and do is yours unconditionally. You may use this power to identify yourself with all that is divine, spiritual, wise, holy, loving, and infinite. You are also free to identify with the illusions of pain, disease, affliction, lack, and limitation.

Create the kind of body that you want to express through the affirmative use of the "I Aм." Affirm the words of Jesus: "I Aм the bread of life" (John 6:48). "I Aм the light of the world" (John 8:12). "I Aм the good shepherd" (John 10:11). "I Aм the resurrection and the life" (John 11:25). "I Aм the way, the truth, and the life" (John 14:6). "I Aм not alone, for my Father is with me" (John 16:32).

From this point forward, resolve to keep the passage to perfect health and wholeness free and clear. Your misuse of the "I Aм" constructs a barrier that will keep the appearances of poor health in your experience. Repeatedly during the next twenty-one days, affirm: *"I AM the Christ."* (It takes twenty-one days to change a thought pattern; however, I believe you can change in an instant.) Affirm this truth with conviction. Choose to block out any thought contrary to this power. Your body will respond with a manifestation equivalent to your conviction.

THE POWER OF A MADE-UP MIND

A certain man went through a forest seeking any bird of interest he might find. He caught a young eagle, brought it home, and put it among the fowls and ducks and turkeys, and gave it chicken food to eat even though it was an eagle, the king of birds.

Five years later, a naturalist came to see him and, after passing through his garden, said: "That bird is an eagle, not a chicken."

"Yes," said the owner, "but I have trained it to be a chicken. It is no longer an eagle, it is a chicken, even though it measures fifteen feet from tip to tip of its wings."

"No," said the naturalist, "it is an eagle still,

it has the heart of an eagle, and I will make it soar high up to the heavens.''

''No,'' said the owner, ''it is a chicken and it will never fly.''

They agreed to test it. The naturalist picked up the eagle, held it up and said with great intensity: ''Eagle, thou art an eagle, thou dost belong to the sky and not to this earth; stretch forth thy wings and fly.''

The eagle turned this way and that, and then looking down, saw the chickens eating their food, and down he jumped.

The owner said, ''I told you it was a chicken.''

''No,'' said the naturalist, ''it is an eagle. Give it another chance tomorrow.''

So the next day he took it to the top of the house and said: ''Eagle, thou art an eagle, stretch forth thy wings and fly.'' But again the eagle, seeing the chickens feeding, jumped down and fed with them.

Then the owner said: ''I told you it was a chicken.''

''No,'' asserted the naturalist, ''it is an eagle, and it has the heart of an eagle; only give it one more chance, and I will make it fly tomorrow.''

The next morning he rose early and took the eagle outside the city and away from the houses, to the foot of a high mountain. The sun was just rising, gilding the top of the mountain with gold, and every crag was glistening in the joy of the beautiful morning.

He picked up the eagle and said to it: "Eagle, thou art an eagle, thou dost belong to the sky and not to the earth; stretch forth thy wings and fly."

The eagle looked around and trembled as if new life were coming to it. Yet it did not fly. The naturalist then made it look straight at the sun. Suddenly it stretched out its wings and, with the screech of an eagle, it mounted higher and higher and never returned. It was an eagle, though it had been kept and trained as a chicken.

We have been created in the image of God, but men have made us think that we are chickens, and so we think we are; but we are eagles. Stretch forth your wings and fly! Don't be content with the food of chickens.*

Get out of that chicken coop right now! You cannot hide from who you really are! You are a unique, unrepeatable, individualized expression of God. The Truth still exists, even though you have chosen to express something else.

*James Aggrey, "Called to Be Eagles," in James S. Hewett, ed., *Illustrations Unlimited* (Wheaton, Ill.: Tyndale House Publishers, 1988).

You do not belong in the barnyard. When you say, "Be careful, because something is going around" or "So-and-So gave his cold to me" or "This pain comes with age" or "Honey, you know this runs in my family" or "This kind of disease is indigenous to my race; I know I will get it"—these are thoughts rooted in a chicken state of mind. I repeat: "Get out of that chicken coop!"

You are capable of doing great things. *You are the world.* Release the lock that you have placed on your mind and summon the Christ in you to come forth. Time has no status in the mind of God. Eliminate the need to punish yourself for unwise choices. *Now is the only time there is!*

THERE IS NOTHING TO FEAR BY CHOOSING LIFE. You are choosing to take the words out of the books, off the pages, and out of the churches. You are choosing to permit the all of God to express through your body as it did in the man sitting by the pool, the woman with the issue of blood, Peter's mother-in-law, the centurion's servant, and Jairus' daughter.

THERE IS NOTHING TO FEAR BY CHOOSING LIFE. You choose to follow your elder brother and Wayshower, Jesus. You choose to bear witness to the truth that you are indeed a *"spiritual being, living in a spiritual world, governed by spiritual laws."* You choose to know that you are in perfect health regardless of the appearances in the body to the contrary. You choose to tune in to God Mind, every day! You choose to acknowledge the Christ in the doctors, nurses, and loving family members. You choose to know that **wherever you are, God is.**

THERE IS NOTHING TO FEAR BY CHOOSING LIFE. You choose to allow the medical profession and others to say what they feel is true. However, you choose to know the truth that you are made of the substance of God. The substance of God is perfect, whole, complete, changeless, and ageless.

The next time the doctor sees you, he will be shocked at what he sees. He will want to know, "Who is this?" Boldly reply, *"I am the Christ, the son of the living God! I know it and I show*

*it! I am in perfect health, because I am health!
I am! I am! I am!''*

TAKE YOUR TRUTH OFF THE SHELF

When you have a physical challenge, your first
inclination is to search for the root cause of the
problem. In human consciousness, the search
leads in the direction of a sympathetic ear. The
good-natured ''ear'' agrees that a ''pity party''
is the perfect relief. The traditional party conversation is, ''Why me? Why this? Why now?
Why? Why? Why?'' The decor is sympathy,
pessimism, doom, and hopelessness.

Misguided exercises such as this occur so easily
during ''valley'' experiences because we have
built a mental shelf where our real nature is
stored. One of the first lessons taught to first-
level Truth students is: *The primary cause of
suffering is forgetting one's divine nature.* To
forget is to disregard, ignore, neglect, omit, and
overlook. When you do not know who you are,

you identify with anything. You become what
you identify with, regardless of what you are.

"I am one with all the wisdom, all the mind, all
the health there is. I and the Father are one. I am
Spirit." The moment you become ill, it is because
you have forgotten these truths about yourself. . . .

Why do you get sick? There are many schools
of thought on this. The medical physicians give
you the material reasons. The psychologists give
you the emotional reasons. The theologian of or-
thodoxy says you become ill because you sin, but
I see so many people sinning who do not get sick
that I am suspicious of that theory. Sometimes
there is no one healthier than a good sinner.

In our Science we say that sickness is a result
of an unconscious negative conditioning over a
period of time. The question which people ply us
with more than any other, and every practitioner
will bear me out in this, is "Why should I have
this illness if I never thought of it?" You didn't
think of it as "it," but you continually thought
of some negative. . . . Illness is the result of
either conscious or subconscious negative conditioning over a period of time. That is what makes
you sick. A consistent change of thought will
make you well, because there is One Process,
One Mind, One Law, and One Good. You are

using It with free will, and you may use It either way you want.*

When you feel that the actions of others have caused some consequence in your life and you resolve to set them straight, you have put your Truth on the shelf. Your belief that outer conditions, whether through people or situations, can affect you is an open invitation for the illusions of pain, sickness, affliction, disease, and suffering to dwell in your body. I cannot say it enough: *You can have only what you are aware of.*

Awareness is described as appreciation, comprehension, knowledge, perception, realization, and understanding. How *aware* are you of resentment, hostility, animosity, irritation, and anger? How *aware* are you of hatred, outrage, fear, worry, or horror? How *aware* are you of spite, envy, rivalry, jealousy, hoarding, and

*From "You Can Be Healthy Today," in *Collected Essays of Raymond Charles Barker* (DeVorss, 1986), pp. 81, 83.

greed? Demonstration of any of the above is another way of putting your Truth on the shelf.

Article after article in newspapers and magazines reports on the adverse effects that thinking of this sort brings into your body. Are these the kinds of traits that you would like to teach to your children? Are these the kinds of traits that you would be happy to see your parents exhibit? Absolutely not! However, these are the causes of disease-creating toxins released in your body. Has your doctor ever said to go home and cultivate hatred, jealousy, envy, and spite as an antidote? The advice is always to think positively, calm down, not to worry, and to display kindness and love.

Love is an attribute of God. Therefore, Love is a quality in *you*. Love is the idea in God Mind of universal oneness. It manifests in you as kindness, benevolence, and compassion. Love attracts. Love draws to you the plan, people, and essentials to facilitate your healing. Love binds. Love connects you to the ever-flowing river of health and wholeness. Love cements. Love joins you to a state of vim, vigor, and vitality. Love harmonizes. Love attunes your thinking, feeling, words, actions, and reactions to the prompting of Spirit.

> There is no difficulty that enough love will not conquer; no disease that enough love will not heal; no door that enough love will not open; no gulf that enough love will not bridge; no wall that enough love will not throw down; no sin that enough love will not redeem.
>
> It makes no difference how deeply seated may be the trouble, how hopeless the outlook, how muddled the tangle, how great the mistake; a sufficient realization of love will dissolve it all. If only you could love enough you would be the happiest and most powerful being in the world.
> —Emmet Fox, *Love*

"Went to the rock for to hide my face,
Rock cried out, 'No hiding-place,
There's no hiding-place down here.'"

CHAPTER 5

Let Go, Let God

ONCE YOU have done all that you know to do, the next step is *release*. As long as you are in possession, in thought, of the concern, it cannot vacate your life. The relief, cure, or healing that you desire already exists. The only delay is your inability to accept it.

Remember: *"There is nothing to heal, only God to be revealed."* The revelation must come through your consciousness. That is where the need is. Continually reliving the description of the symptoms and the doctor's diagnosis; discussing it all, detail by detail with others; and listening to others share their ordeal with you, binds you to the disease.

Cease to recognize anything less than pefection in anyone you encounter. Otherwise the belief in pain, sickness, and disease will be lodged in your soul consciousness. These illusions will then remain in your body, life, and affairs. When the subject of disease is discussed, direct the conversation to uplifting, positive words of wholeness, health, and perfection.

Rather than participating in useless conversation about "how bad he looks," ***affirm that the healing power of God is released in every cell of the affected part.*** If you cannot perceive wholeness in others, it cannot manifest in you.

Whether you are in a hospital, at home, or with family members, you are on holy ground. This ground only brings forth crops of energy, strength, vivaciousness, and well-being. ***Banish***

all fear about your seeming condition. I say *seeming*, because its only image is in your mind.

Let the regenerative power of life break forth inside of you. Feel it permeate every cell, fiber, organ, muscle, and tissue of your being. Advise the cells of your body to relax and allow the allness of God to restore them to their original state.

This is the day of your spiritual breakthrough. It does not matter what the need is, **"God will take care of you."**

THE PRAYER OF FAITH

God is my help in every need;
God does my every hunger feed;
God walks beside me, guides my way
Through every moment of this day.

I now am wise, I now am true,
Patient, kind, and loving, too.

All things I am, can do, and be,
Through Christ, the Truth that is in me.

God is my health, I can't be sick;
God is my strength, unfailing, quick;
God is my all, I know no fear,
Since God and love and Truth are here.

—Hannah More Kohaus

We hope you have enjoyed
this book and invite you to consider
reading other books from DeVorss Publications
by calling 800.843.5743 for a free copy of our catalog.
We will gladly send the information you need
to help you along your spiritual journey.

Thank You!